THE AMAZING HUMAN BODY

THE HUMAN
DIGESTIVE SYSTEM
by Sue Bradford Edwards

BrightPoint Press

San Diego, CA

BrightP◆int Press

© 2025 BrightPoint Press
an imprint of ReferencePoint Press, Inc.
Printed in the United States

For more information, contact:
BrightPoint Press
PO Box 27779
San Diego, CA 92198
www.BrightPointPress.com

ALL RIGHTS RESERVED.

No part of this work covered by the copyright hereon may be reproduced or used in any form or by any means—graphic, electronic, or mechanical, including photocopying, recording, taping, web distribution, or information storage retrieval systems—without the written permission of the publisher.

LIBRARY OF CONGRESS CATALOGING-IN-PUBLICATION DATA

Name: Edwards, Sue Bradford, author.
Title: The human digestive system / by Sue Bradford Edwards.
Description: San Diego, CA: BrightPoint Press, 2025 | Series: The amazing human body |
  Audience: Grade 7 to 9 | Includes bibliographical references and index.
Identifiers: ISBN: 9781678209582 (hardcover) | ISBN: 9781678209599 (eBook)
The complete Library of Congress record is available at www.loc.gov.

CONTENTS

AT A GLANCE   4

INTRODUCTION   6
LIVING WITH IRRITABLE BOWEL SYNDROME

CHAPTER ONE   12
WHAT IS THE DIGESTIVE SYSTEM?

CHAPTER TWO   22
HOW DOES THE DIGESTIVE SYSTEM WORK?

CHAPTER THREE   36
WHAT CAN GO WRONG WITH THE
DIGESTIVE SYSTEM?

CHAPTER FOUR   48
WHAT CAN HUMANS DO TO KEEP THE
DIGESTIVE SYSTEM HEALTHY?

Glossary   58
Source Notes   59
For Further Research   60
Index   62
Image Credits   63
About the Author   64

AT A GLANCE

- Food is the body's source of energy.

- Digestion makes it possible for the body to use the nutrients in food.

- The digestive system is a group of organs in the human body that digest food.

- As food passes through the digestive system, the body breaks it down into smaller parts.

- The body absorbs much of the nutrients in food in the small intestine. Then, food passes through the large intestine before being released as waste.

- Muscles contract and relax to push food through the digestive system.

- Constipation, diarrhea, and gas can all be symptoms of digestive conditions. Many of these conditions can be treated.

- Cancers are among the most serious digestive conditions. Many cancers can be treated.

- Eating well, getting enough sleep, and exercising help keep the digestive system healthy.

INTRODUCTION

LIVING WITH IRRITABLE BOWEL SYNDROME

Emma always had digestive problems. As a child, she often had stomachaches. They would pass quickly. She didn't worry too much about them.

Then, in second grade, she caught a virus. It made her throw up in class. Even after getting better, she panicked whenever her stomach hurt. She didn't want to get sick in front of other people again.

Stomachaches are common and are not always a sign of a serious problem. However, people should talk to a doctor if a stomachache is severe or long-lasting.

Constipation is a side effect of many different kinds of medications.

Emma's mother was a nurse for children. She knew that worrying can make a person feel sick. To help relieve Emma's fear, she made Emma a bracelet. It said, "Power Through." Whenever Emma worried, she looked at the bracelet. It helped her calm down.

Then, in high school, Emma had acne. Her doctor gave her a medication to clear up her skin. One side effect of the medication was constipation. This meant that Emma didn't go to the bathroom as often as she should. Sometimes this made her feel queasy. She began to worry more than she had before.

One night, she had severe pain. Her parents took her to the hospital. Doctors looked at her intestines and stomach. An X-ray showed that **stool** filled Emma's intestines. The doctors **diagnosed** her with irritable bowel syndrome (IBS). This disorder causes pain, constipation, and diarrhea.

Doctors don't know why people get IBS. But they do have ways of treating it. Emma's doctors gave her medications to fight the constipation and reduce her pain. They told her to eat small meals several times a day. They also told her to exercise regularly. This treatment plan helped Emma avoid straining her digestive system. She says, "I'm not anxious about my stomach now because I know what to do. I have a plan."[1]

THE DIGESTIVE SYSTEM

The digestive system is a group of organs in the body. These organs break down food into smaller parts. This process is called digestion. The body uses digested food to fuel itself and to grow.

Some people have problems with their digestive systems. IBS is one kind of digestive disorder. It affects the stomach

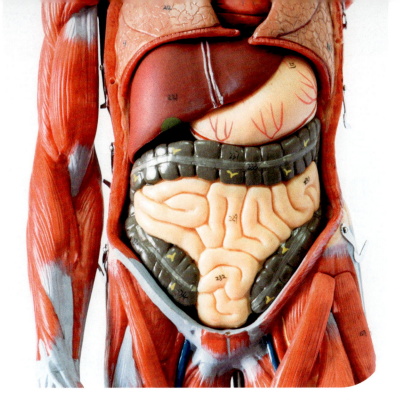

Most of the digestive system's organs are located in the abdomen, or belly.

and intestines. Other conditions affect different parts of the digestive system, such as the mouth and esophagus.

Fortunately, doctors can treat many digestive problems. There are also things people can do to keep their digestive systems healthy. It all starts with knowing what the digestive system is and how it works.

CHAPTER ONE

WHAT IS THE DIGESTIVE SYSTEM?

The digestive system breaks food down into nutrients. Nutrients are substances that living things need to survive. Nutrients give the body energy. They also help the body grow and heal.

Carbohydrates are one kind of nutrient. They include sugars and **fiber**. The body uses these nutrients for energy. Foods such as grains and fruits are high

All living things must take in energy in order to survive. Humans are able to eat food from a variety of sources, including plants and animals.

Most packaged food sold in the United States is labeled with information about the nutrients it contains.

in carbohydrates. So are certain vegetables, such as potatoes and corn.

Proteins are another kind of nutrient. Foods such as meat, eggs, and beans are high in proteins. Each protein performs a specific task for living things. For example, the protein lactase helps people digest milk.

Proteins are large **molecules**. During digestion, proteins are broken into smaller molecules. These smaller molecules are called amino acids. The body makes new proteins out of amino acids.

Fats are also a kind of nutrient. The body uses fats as an energy source. Fats also help the body absorb other nutrients. Fats can come from oils such as olive oil and

Calories

The energy in food is measured in calories. Some foods are higher in calories than others. Foods high in fats and carbohydrates tend to be high in calories. Sausages, nuts, and cake are examples of high-calorie foods. Vegetables are usually lower in calories. This is because vegetables are mostly water and fiber.

sunflower oil. Digestion breaks fats into fatty acids. The body uses fatty acids in many ways, including as an energy source.

Vitamins and minerals are nutrients too. Vitamins are **organic** substances. The body needs vitamins in small amounts. Vitamins play many different roles in the body. For example, vitamin C helps the body heal wounds. Minerals are inorganic substances. The body needs them in small amounts too. For example, people need the mineral calcium to keep their bones healthy.

GETTING TO THE ENERGY

For the body to use nutrients, food must be broken down. The teeth crush the food. Muscles in the digestive system squeeze

Like people and other animals, plants need nutrients too. They absorb some nutrients from the soil through their roots.

the food. This squeezing stirs and mixes the food with digestive juices. These juices also break down the food.

When the food has been broken down, the body can use its nutrients. These nutrients give the body energy. Everything the body does requires energy. It uses energy to move, grow, and heal.

Food is the body's source of energy. Almost all the energy in food originally comes from the sun. Plants pull in water. They also pull in a gas called carbon dioxide. Plants combine these ingredients with the sun's energy to make a carbohydrate called glucose. This process is called photosynthesis. Animals that eat plants digest the glucose and other nutrients. This gives them energy.

Cells do not use glucose itself as energy. Instead, they change it into energy the body can use. This is done through a process called cellular respiration. In some ways, respiration is the opposite of photosynthesis. First, the cells bring together glucose and oxygen. This makes water and carbon dioxide. This process also releases energy. This is the energy that cells use.

HOW THE NERVOUS SYSTEM HELPS

Digestion happens with help from the nervous system. The nervous system includes the brain, the spinal cord, and

Nerves send messages to other parts of the body using chemical and electrical signals.

the nerves. The spinal cord runs from the brain down through the spine. Nerves branch off from the spinal cord. The nerves allow the brain to send messages to the rest of the body.

The body's senses use nerves to take in information about the world. For example, nerves in the nose send messages to the

A person smells something when small particles from the thing being smelled activate nerve cells deep inside the nose.

brain in response to the smell of food. "Your nervous system picks up millions of bits of information," says Professor Mike Todorovic.[2] He explains that the brain reviews the information. It decides what the body should do next. Then it sends a signal to the parts of the body needed to do the job.

Digestion could not happen without the nervous system. Nerves tell the body when to release digestive juices. Other nerves activate when the stomach is empty. They tell muscles to relax. This allows food to enter the stomach. Nerves also react when the stomach is full. They tell stomach muscles when to squeeze the food. Nerves also tell the muscles to push the food through the digestive system.

CHAPTER TWO

HOW DOES THE DIGESTIVE SYSTEM WORK?

The digestive system starts working even before people take a bite of food. First, people see or smell food. Their salivary glands start working. Glands are organs. They make and release substances that do jobs for the body. The salivary glands make saliva, or spit. Saliva is the first digestive juice.

The mouth is the first part of the digestive system. This is where the body

The average person produces 17 to 51 fluid ounces (0.5 to 1.5 L) of saliva per day.

begins to break down food. The teeth grind the food into smaller pieces. Saliva mixes with the food. Saliva contains **enzymes**. One is called amylase. It breaks down carbohydrates.

DOWN THE ESOPHAGUS

Once people are finished chewing, they swallow the food. The tongue pushes it into the throat. The food enters the esophagus. This is a long, narrow tube made of muscles. The muscles behind the food squeeze. The muscles ahead of the food relax. This wavelike motion is called peristalsis. It pushes food through the digestive system.

The food reaches the end of the esophagus. A strong ring of muscle stops the food's progress. This ring is called a sphincter. It opens to let food into the stomach. Then it squeezes shut again. This keeps the contents of the stomach from returning to the esophagus.

The stomach is an organ shaped like the letter *J*. It is in the left center of the abdomen. In the stomach, muscles squeeze

Salivating for Sour Candy

Some people like sour candy. When they eat it, their mouth may ache. These aches may happen near the jaw hinge or at the base of their mouth. The salivary glands cause these aches. The glands make lots of saliva in response to sour things. This is because sour things are acidic. The saliva reduces the acid's strength. This helps protect the body.

When a person is hungry, the stomach may make a deep, rumbling sound. This happens when the muscles in the stomach contract.

to stir the food. Digestive juices mix with the food. These juices include enzymes and stomach acid. The juices break down the food into even smaller pieces. The stomach holds the food for between 40 minutes and 2 hours. Then the food passes further into the digestive system.

Once empty, the stomach shrinks. It expands when more food enters it. The stomach can change its shape because it is lined with folded body tissue. Jonathan Bennion teaches at the Institute of Human Anatomy. He explains the purpose of this tissue. He says, "These folds are called gastric rugae and they allow for your stomach to stretch when you decide to continue to eat."[3]

The food becomes a thick liquid as it is digested. This liquid is called chyme. At the base of the stomach is the pylorus. This part contains another sphincter. It opens to let the chyme into the small intestine.

ABSORBING AND EXPELLING

The intestine is a long tube made of muscles that begins after the stomach. It is divided into the small intestine and the large intestine. The small intestine is located beneath the stomach. Despite its name, the small intestine is not very small. "If you were to stretch out your small intestine, it would be about three times your height," says Nancy Bullard.[4] Bullard is an award-winning science teacher. She says the organ is

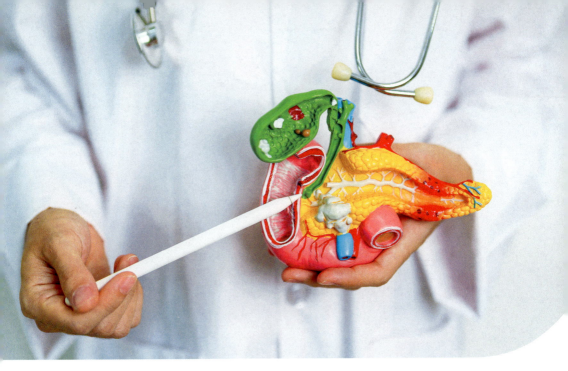

Besides digestive juices, the pancreas (modeled in yellow) also produces insulin. This substance helps control the level of sugar in the blood.

called the small intestine because it is narrower than the large intestine.

The small intestine continues to break down food. It has three sections. The first is the duodenum. This is where the body first begins to absorb the nutrients from the food. The pancreas and liver release digestive juices into the duodenum.

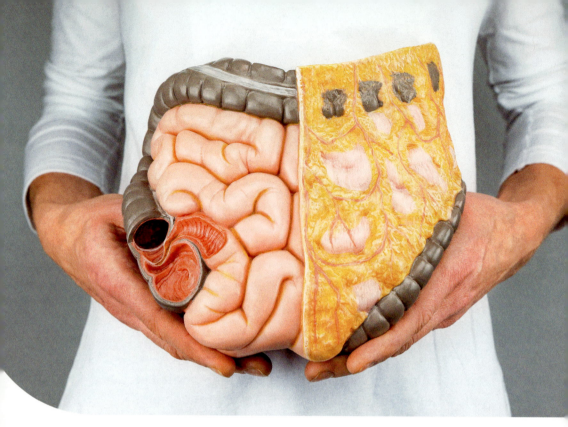

The small intestine (modeled in pink) holds food for about 5 hours.

The pancreas is an organ that makes juices that break down nutrients. The liver is an organ that produces bile. Bile helps digest fats and some vitamins. Some bile is stored in an organ called the gallbladder. Bile can also be passed directly into the small intestine. Water from the bloodstream is also pulled into the small intestines. Water helps absorb nutrients. It also helps the chyme move through the intestines smoothly.

The second section of the small intestine is the jejunum. Villi line this section. Villi are small, hairlike structures. They give the small intestine more surface area. This means there is more contact between the body and the chyme. The villi contain tiny blood vessels. The jejunum is deep red in color because of these blood vessels. The vessels absorb nutrients from the chyme. Then the blood carries the nutrients throughout the body.

The final section is the ileum. This is the longest section of the small intestine.

Food spends more time in the ileum than in the other two sections. Bacteria live in the ileum. Bacteria are single-celled living things. They live almost everywhere in the world. This includes inside the human digestive system. Some intestinal bacteria make useful enzymes. The enzymes help break down chyme.

Peristalsis pushes the chyme through the small intestine. The chyme moves through another sphincter. It enters the large intestine. The sphincter closes. This keeps the chyme from returning to the small intestine.

The chyme in the large intestine has mostly been digested. But there is still more to be done. Bacteria that live in the large intestine break down the chyme

The small intestine has about 6,000 to 25,000 villi per square inch (930 to 3,900 per sq cm).

THE HUMAN DIGESTIVE SYSTEM

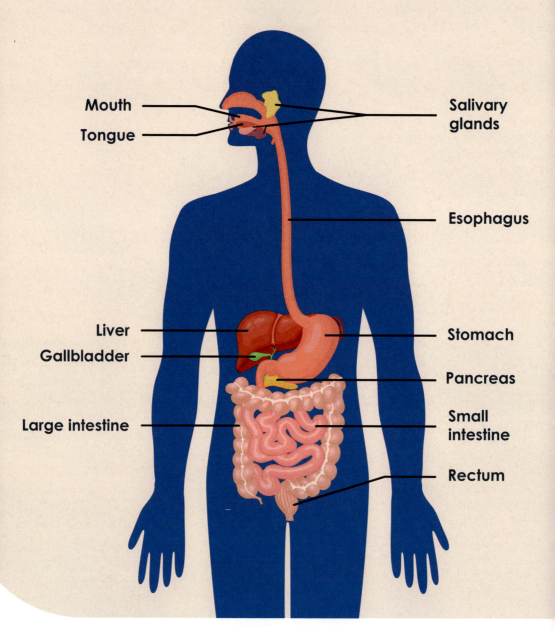

This diagram shows where the parts of the digestive system are located in the body.

even further. These bacteria also make vitamin K. Vitamin K helps the blood clot. This is how the body stops bleeding. Clotting makes scabs form. Vitamin K also helps build bones.

The large intestine has another job. It absorbs water from the chyme. This water returns to the bloodstream. As water is removed, the chyme becomes solid. This solid waste is now stool. It is stored in the rectum until the person passes the stool. It takes about 36 hours for the contents of the large intestine to pass through it.

CHAPTER THREE

WHAT CAN GO WRONG WITH THE DIGESTIVE SYSTEM?

Many diseases, injuries, and other issues affect the digestive system. Each of these issues can produce different symptoms. People may have bloating. This happens when gas, liquid, or other substances cause the stomach or intestines to swell. Constipation and diarrhea can also occur. Nausea is a common symptom. Nausea can lead to vomiting, or throwing up.

Doctors who treat problems with the digestive system are called gastroenterologists.

Sometimes these symptoms do not have serious causes. Other times, they may be signs of serious issues. People should pay attention to how their digestive system feels. They should talk to a doctor if they have concerns.

COMMON DIGESTIVE PROBLEMS

One common problem is gas. The digestive system produces gas as it breaks down food. Too much gas can make the stomach or abdomen hurt. To relieve this feeling, people burp or fart. One cause of gas is swallowing air by eating too fast. Another cause is a change in diet. Eating more fiber than usual can briefly cause gas.

Another common problem is constipation. Constipation happens

Bacteria in the large intestine produce gas as they break down food. This can contribute to a bloating feeling.

when people have trouble making bowel movements. They may have fewer than usual. Or they may have difficult or painful bowel movements. Constipation can have many causes. Sometimes the food people eat briefly causes constipation. Certain diseases can also cause this issue. For example, people with celiac disease may

Grain plants produce gluten to help them grow. In bread, gluten gives the food a stretchy, chewy quality.

get constipated when they eat gluten. This is a protein found in some grains.

People with celiac disease have trouble digesting gluten. Their body mistakes gluten for something harmful. The body responds by trying to destroy it. This can cause a range of symptoms. Some people have no symptoms. Others have diarrhea or constipation. Some might have abdominal pain or gas. They might also have nausea. Celiac disease can even damage the small intestine. To diagnose celiac disease, a doctor may order a blood test. The doctor might also look at a **biopsy** from the small intestine.

Diarrhea is another common digestive issue. Diarrhea is loose or watery stool that

Foodborne Illnesses

Sometimes food contains harmful substances or bacteria. If someone eats this food, they can get sick. This sickness is called a foodborne illness. One common symptom is a fever. Diarrhea and nausea are also common. More serious cases can lead to blurred vision. Muscle weakness or paralysis is also possible. Improperly cooked food is a common cause of foodborne illness.

happens at least three times in one day. Like constipation, diarrhea can have many causes. Some viruses can cause it. Certain medications can also cause diarrhea. People can get diarrhea after eating a food their body cannot digest. Doctors tell people with diarrhea to drink fluids. Diarrhea can also be treated with medication.

Some people suffer from acid reflux. This is a digestive problem in which stomach acid enters the esophagus. Acid reflux causes heartburn. This feels like a painful burning in the chest. Acid reflux can happen when people eat before bed. When they lie down, the contents of the stomach slide into the esophagus. Acid reflux may also happen after people eat certain things. For example, spicy food can cause acid reflux.

Despite its name, heartburn does not affect the heart.

Irritable bowel syndrome (IBS) is another digestive issue. It affects 10 to 15 percent of people. It causes abdominal pain. It also causes changes in the stool. One day a person with IBS might be constipated. The next, they may have diarrhea. IBS is hard to diagnose. The doctor must rule out other problems first. Registered nurse Cathy Parkes says, "Treatment of IBS includes diet changes, lifestyle changes, as well as medications. Diet changes that can be helpful include increasing your fiber intake as well as avoiding gluten."[5]

SERIOUS DIGESTIVE PROBLEMS

Some digestive system problems can be serious. Hernias are one such problem. A hernia happens when a person has a weak place in the muscles of their abdomen. A gap forms in the muscle. Fat can poke through the gap. So can part of the small intestine.

An untreated hernia can be dangerous. If a hernia is not treated, blood flow can be cut off. This can lead to a strangulated hernia. This happens when the tissue pushing through the gap is pinched.

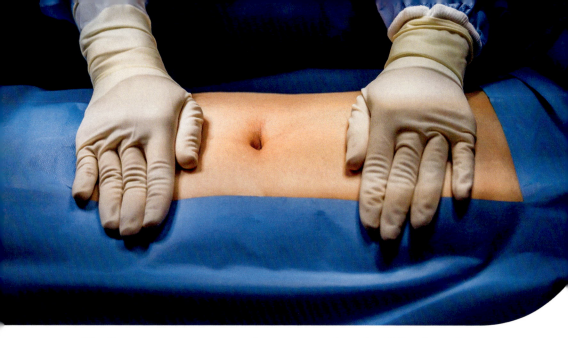

Each year, surgeons perform more than 1 million hernia surgeries in the United States. It is one of the most common surgeries in the country.

Then the tissue dies. One sign of a strangulated hernia is intense pain. Another is redness around the hernia. The bulge may also get bigger. This condition can be deadly. Surgery can fix it.

Some of the most serious digestive diseases are cancers. Cancer is when there is unusual cell growth in the body. This can lead to the growth of a tumor. Digestive system cancers are named after where the tumor grows. For example, stomach cancer is in the stomach.

Men are more likely to get digestive system cancers than women. People who smoke are at higher risk. So are those

Some digestive system cancers are treated with radiation therapy. This treatment uses machines that create powerful waves of energy to kill the cancer.

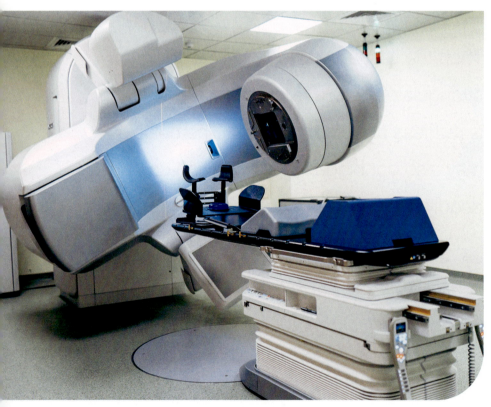

who drink alcohol. An unhealthy diet also increases risk. Cancer can be fatal. However, many digestive system cancers can be treated. Surgery can cut out a tumor. Medications and special treatments can keep the cancer from growing. Treatments can prolong the lives of people with cancer.

CHAPTER FOUR

WHAT CAN HUMANS DO TO KEEP THE DIGESTIVE SYSTEM HEALTHY?

Eating well is one of the most important things people can do to keep their digestive system healthy. Eating well can mean different things for different people. Culture and personal tastes affect people's diets. There is no one right way to eat. Instead, doctors say people should follow broad guidelines when choosing what to eat.

Food is a central part of cultures around the world. Effective healthy eating advice considers how culture influences the way people eat.

Avoiding eating ultra-processed foods is a good place to start. These foods contain many unnatural ingredients. Companies add these ingredients to make food tastier. They also add them to make food last longer before spoiling. However, ultra-processed foods are usually less healthy than less processed foods. Examples of ultra-processed foods include sugary drinks, frozen meals, and potato chips. Doctors say that people should limit these kinds of foods in their diets.

One thing that helps many people eat well is cooking at home. People can cook healthy meals themselves using minimally processed foods. Cooking at home requires time. It also requires knowledge, healthy food, and cooking tools. It may not always be easy or possible for people to cook healthy meals at home. Doctors say that people should start small when changing their diets. That way, they can make lasting changes that work for them.

Food from restaurants usually contains high amounts of salt, fats, and calories. This can make it less healthy than home-cooked food. Cooking at home allows people to control the ingredients in their food.

Tofu is made from soybeans. This food is a healthy, nonmeat source of protein.

HEALTHY FOODS

Fresh vegetables and fruits are the basis of many healthy diets. These foods are high in fiber. Fiber helps keep the gut healthy. Many people lack fiber in their diets. "Americans' fiber intake is 40 to 50 percent of what it should be," says Dr. Gerard Mullin.[6]

Sources of protein are another important part of a healthy diet. Some foods are very high in protein. These include meat, beans, nuts, and dairy. Healthy sources of protein include salmon, chicken, lentils, and tempeh.

Fermented foods can also be healthy. People ferment foods by adding special kinds of **microbes** to them. The microbes alter the food's chemistry. This changes how they taste. It also allows them to last longer without spoiling. Some fermented foods contain probiotics. These are microbes that help the human

Probiotics

Probiotics help the body digest food. They might also fend off microbes that are bad for digestion. Yeast and some bacteria are probiotics. People can buy foods and medicines with probiotics in them. Yogurt is a food that commonly has probiotics.

digestive system. Kefir is a fermented milk drink. It is a lot like yogurt. It is full of probiotics. Another fermented food is sourdough bread. Sauerkraut and kimchi are fermented foods made from cabbage.

OTHER WAYS TO HELP

Eating well is important for digestive health. But there are other things people can do to keep the digestive system healthy. Getting enough sleep is important. Lack of sleep can lead to stress. The digestive system is sensitive to stress. This is because the brain and gut communicate using nerve cells.

Stress can cause a variety of symptoms in the digestive system. One symptom is heartburn. Dr. Muhammad Talha Farooqui explains, "Stress can slow down digestion, keeping food in your stomach longer, which can be a trigger for heartburn."[7]

The Centers for Disease Control and Prevention (CDC) is a US government agency. The CDC has a list of ways people can reduce stress. Physical activity is one of them. The CDC recommends 10-minute walks and other small exercises. The CDC

Exercise can draw blood away from the digestive system and to other muscles. People should not exercise right after eating a large meal.

says that people should be active for 2.5 hours each week. The CDC also points out that laughter can help reduce stress. It recommends thinking of something funny or watching a funny online video. The CDC reminds people to take breaks when doing something stressful as well.

People also need to drink plenty of water. Water is necessary for all of the body's functions. This includes digestion. Digestive juices contain water. Water helps the body absorb nutrients. Not getting enough water can cause constipation and other issues.

THE IMPORTANCE OF HEALTHY DIGESTION

The digestive system does an important job. It turns food into energy. First it breaks

The digestive system helps children and teens grow.

food down. Then it absorbs nutrients. It also helps remove waste that the body cannot use.

Things can go wrong with the digestive system. But there are steps people can take to keep it healthy. Eating well, getting enough sleep, and exercising all contribute to digestive health.

GLOSSARY

biopsy

a medical test that is performed on a sample of tissue or cells

cells

the basic units of living things

diagnosed

determined the cause of a medical condition

enzymes

substances that promote the chemical reactions occurring within living things

fiber

a type of carbohydrate that helps the body digest food but is not digested itself

microbes

very small living things that cannot be seen by the naked eye

molecules

groups of atoms bound together that form a pure chemical substance

organic

related to living things

stool

solid human waste, also known as poop

SOURCE NOTES

INTRODUCTION: LIVING WITH IRRITABLE BOWEL SYNDROME

1. Quoted in "Irritable Bowel Syndrome: Emma's Story," *Children's Hospital of Philadelphia*, September 11, 2018. www.chop.edu.

CHAPTER ONE: WHAT IS THE DIGESTIVE SYSTEM?

2. Quoted in Dr Matt & Dr Mike, "Introduction to the Nervous System," *YouTube*, July 30, 2020. www.youtube.com.

CHAPTER TWO: HOW DOES THE DIGESTIVE SYSTEM WORK?

3. Quoted in Institute of Human Anatomy, "Looking Inside a Real Human Stomach," *YouTube*, August 11, 2022. www.youtube.com.

4. Nancy Bullard, "The Digestive System Is Amazing!," *YouTube*, August 22, 2023. www.youtube.com.

CHAPTER THREE: WHAT CAN GO WRONG WITH THE DIGESTIVE SYSTEM?

5. Quoted in Level Up RN, "Irritable Bowel Syndrome (IBS): Symptoms & Treatments - Ask A Nurse," *YouTube*, March 19, 2023. www.youtube.com.

CHAPTER FOUR: WHAT CAN HUMANS DO TO KEEP THE DIGESTIVE SYSTEM HEALTHY?

6. Quoted in "Your Digestive System: 5 Ways to Support Gut Health," *Johns Hopkins Medicine*, n.d. www.hopkinsmedicine.org.

7. Quoted in "How Does Stress Affect the Digestive System?," *Houston Methodist*, February 15, 2023. www.houstonmethodist.org.

FOR FURTHER RESEARCH

BOOKS

Leigh McClure, *The Digestive System.* Buffalo, NY: Rosen, 2024.

Elaine Skiadas, *Fantastic Vegan Recipes for the Teen Cook*. Salem, MA: Page Street, 2023.

Chelsea Xie, *The Human Circulatory System*. San Diego, CA: BrightPoint Press, 2025.

INTERNET SOURCES

"Healthy Eating Plate," *Harvard T.H. Chan School of Public Health*, January 2023. https://nutritionsource.hsph.harvard.edu.

"How Your Digestive System Works," *Gastroenterology Consultants of San Antonio*, April 19, 2022. www.gastroconsa.com.

Shawn Khodadadian, "How Exercise Affects Your Digestion," *Manhattan Gastroenterology*, August 27, 2022. www.manhattangastroenterology.com.

WEBSITES

Mayo Clinic
www.mayoclinic.org

The Mayo Clinic provides a variety of health information on its website, including about the digestive system.

MedlinePlus
www.medlineplus.gov

MedlinePlus is an official website of the US government. It provides information on health topics and healthy eating.

Nutrition.gov
www.nutrition.gov

This official website of the US government offers trustworthy information on nutrition.

INDEX

acid reflux, 42, 54–55
amino acids, 15

bacteria, 32–35, 41, 53
bile, 30
bloating, 36–38

calories, 15
cancer, 45–47
carbohydrates, 12–15, 18, 24
celiac disease, 39–41
cellular respiration, 18–19
chyme, 28, 31–35
constipation, 9–10, 36–40,
    42-43, 56

diarrhea, 9, 36, 40–43
digestive juices, 17, 21, 22, 27,
    29–30, 56

eating well, 48–54, 57
esophagus, 11, 24–25, 34, 42

fats, 15–16, 30
fiber, 12, 15, 38, 44, 52
foodborne illnesses, 41

gallbladder, 30, 34
gastric rugae, 27
glucose, 18

hernias, 44–45

irritable bowel syndrome (IBS),
    9–11, 43–44

large intestine, 28–29, 32–35
liver, 29–30, 34

minerals, 16

nausea, 36, 41
nervous system, 19–21, 54

pancreas, 29–30, 34
peristalsis, 21, 24, 32
probiotics, 53–54
proteins, 14–15, 40, 52–53

saliva, 22–25
small intestine, 28–34, 41, 44
sphincter, 25, 28, 32
stomach, 6, 9–10, 21, 25–28, 34,
    36–38, 42, 46, 55
stool, 9, 35, 41–43
stress, 54–56

ultra-processed foods, 50

villi, 31
vitamins, 16, 30, 35
vomiting, 6, 36, 41

IMAGE CREDITS

Cover: © FOTOGRAFIA INC./iStockphoto

5: © Twinsterphoto/Shutterstock Images

7: © comodigit/Shutterstock Images

8: © PeopleImages.com - Yuri A/Shutterstock Images

11: © Komsan Loonprom/Shutterstock Images

13: © Stephanie Frey/Shutterstock Images

14: © Rix Pix Photography/Shutterstock Images

17: © fotohunter/Shutterstock Images

19: © Billion Photos/Shutterstock Images

20: © New Africa/Shutterstock Images

23: © Seler.up/Shutterstock Images

26: © Mallika Home Studio/Shutterstock Images

29: © Jo Panuwat D/Shutterstock Images

30: © Ben Schonewille/Shutterstock Images

33: © Daniel Oakfield/Shutterstock Images

34: © Valentina Antuganova/Shutterstock Images

37: © Ground Picture/Shutterstock Images

39: © Red Stock/Shutterstock Images

40: © New Africa/Shutterstock Images

43: © 9nong/Shutterstock Images

45: © Peter Porrini/Shutterstock Images

46: © My Ocean Production/Shutterstock Images

49: © wavebreakmedia/Shutterstock Images

51: © Dean Drobot/Shutterstock Images

52: © Nungning20/Shutterstock Images

55: © Master of Stocks/Shutterstock Images

57: © diplomedia/Shutterstock Images

ABOUT THE AUTHOR

Sue Bradford Edwards is a nonfiction author who lives in St. Louis, Missouri. She has written more than fifty books for young readers. Her health-related titles include *Fats, Robotics in Health Care, Stem Cells, Meth, Steroids,* and *What Are Learning Disorders?* She and her son visit the markets near home to find new fruits and vegetables to try.